WHY ARE YOU NOT RICH?

The Question
That Silenced The Room

Four Barriers To Financial Independence

~   I0143264

WALTER A. AIKENS

AOCSI.org

Other Books by Walter A. Aikens

≈

Scattered Pieces of a Broken Dream

The Purpose of Knowledge

The Lifespan of a Moment

The Art of Cultivating Social Intelligence

WHY ARE YOU NOT RICH?

The Question
That Silenced The Room

AOCSI.org

In Association with

Lulu.

Cover Design by Freedom Jovan Graves

Back Cover Photo

By

Rondell Lane of Media Lane Photo and Video

Dedicated to Pastor Otis Lockett Sr.

This book is dedicated to the phenomenal Pastor Otis Lockett Sr. The man who refused to allow black underachievement (or any underachievement) to go unchallenged. Thank you for targeting minority males and daring them to raise their expectations of themselves. You were bold enough to ask, "Why are you not rich?" The question did indeed, silence the entire room. You were patient enough to wait until every willing voice had an opportunity to be heard. The investment you made in me was for the benefit of the world. Thank you for challenging me to become a better me, and men to become better men.

Walter A. Aikens

Acknowledgements

The writer would like to thank William Scott Holloway for his mentorship in developing creative ways to disseminate valuable information. The lovely Tanya Mizell for demanding to hear the story of, "The question that silenced the room," over and over and over again until this book was conceived. Thanks to my son Freedom Jovan for the cover design. Thanks to Tioko Holmes, my website designer for being my yellow line that kept me from crossing into oncoming traffic. Thanks to Media Lane Photography for making me look better than I actually do. Thanks to Derick Virgil for insisting that I publish this book "right now." And last but far from least, thanks to my fantastic and beautiful wife of twenty five years, Faith R. Aikens. Several years ago for our anniversary I got her a trophy.

That should say it all.

Table of Contents

Introduction

THE QUESTION THAT SILENCED THE ROOM
"WHY ARE YOU NOT RICH?"

The question was asked by a Pastor to a group of minority men. The question silenced the room. The men looked at the pastor as the pastor looked at the men, in return. Surely this is a rhetorical question, not expected to be answered. No one said a word. The silence was so loud it was deafening. Then the men realized the pastor was waiting for an answer. One bold soul offered in a slow unsteady voice his answer to the question. The discourse had begun.

The question asked by the facilitator segued into an interesting discussion concerning some fundamental flaws prominent in the financial sphere of many minority and African American men; economics: "Why the monetary disparity between European American, Asian American and African American men?" The answer to the original question "Why are you not rich?" which was offered by the writer in response, has become the spark to address the following: four barriers to financial independence.

If an individual will self-assess themselves by seriously considering the weighty implications of this odd question ("Why are you not rich?"), one may come up with a myriad of reasons varying in range and scope, other than the reasons listed in this material. The author has tried (to no avail) to locate the audio of the initial meeting in which this subject silenced men of minority status and forced them into deep thought and contemplation. In other words, you may have four or more entirely different reasons for not having realized a level of financial security, independence, liberty, sustenance, etc., etc. Your reason may be singularly: "Because I don't want to be rich." That is your prerogative. But if a man reaches the age of forty, in a capitalist society called America, he could be (in my weird opinion) expected to be asked and should be prepared to answer this question, WHY ARE YOU NOT RICH?

The man that sparked the debate would have turned 61 February 28 2015. He transitioned several years ago and this treatise is a part of his legacy. He once stated, "If your dream can be realized in your life time, it's not big enough." Since I never dreamed of asking or being asked the question "why are you not rich?," I will concede this writing is connected with his vision, more so than mine. The devotion he had to success was intimidating, the love and concern he had for empowering others was unquestionable. The underlying issue appears to be; why, in a land of plenty, a land of opportunity, and a land of wealth, are so many minority men underrepresented in the status of financial independence. Keys to accumulating wealth are not complicated. But to achieve wealth (particularly for the uninitiated), may require the removal of certain barriers that we may all face at one time or another in our lives. Four primary barriers will be addressed here. This discussion is dedicated to the man that had the audacity to confront men, (traditionally associated with underachievement), with one of the toughest questions ever encountered; why are you not rich?

Chapter I

FEAR

"If you live in America and you are poor, it's your fault."
Herman Cain, 2012 Presidential Candidate

Are you afraid to make money? You should be. It's illegal...it's called counterfeiting. Are you afraid to create wealth? That's a better question. Being afraid to create wealth is a different thing all together. Several terms of financial literacy should be noted and studied in order to take part in a serious conversation concerning wealth. Many terms used in today's financial discourse are misunderstood by the general public. And many terms have taken on new meanings over a vast expanse of time.

In a capitalist society money is initially earned. Rich is a general term many take for granted without fully understanding what it implies. Wealth is another misunderstood concept. These are terms that need to be examined if we are to get to the underlying cause of why so many lack access to the principles that generate true wealth. Before researching these terms hear this. Money is earned. Or it should be, if its acquisition is to be respected. Currency is printed or minted and has to be sanctioned by the Federal Reserve, to be considered legal tender in the United States of America.

While working as a therapist with a client that had a history of relapsing into drug use, the topic of fear came up. The conversation progressed to the fear of failure and the fear of success. The client appeared to sink into a deep emotional abyss, rubbed his hand across his face and said, "I have a fear of failure." Without thinking of the potential impact my words would have, I replied, "No, you don't have a fear of failure, you are too good at it (failure). You have a fear of success." I had his undivided attention.

How does one differentiate between the fear of failure and the fear of success? My personal yard stick is this; a person who has a fear of failure will rarely start anything. A person with a fear of success will rarely finish anything. Fear has the ability to freeze our efforts and rob us of confidence. Most live beneath the poverty level and have no experience managing money. The game of Monopoly is excellent for experiencing gain and lost. Baseball is a good parallel for risk management. Chess, however, is the closest life parallel that may expose a person to facing consequences without the element of "luck." People expecting to luck up and find a fortune are never going to successfully harness the courage to manage wealth. That is why some gamblers adopt the easy come easy go philosophy. Chess outcomes are determined by choice. There is no roll of the dice and hope something lands on a particular space. In chess you must choose the piece you intend to move, you must choose where you intend to place that piece, and the move is not complete until you let go of the man. Fear is a natural emotion but needs to be understood in its proper context.

How Does One Overcome Fear?

Most financially troubled individuals are not afraid to earn money, not afraid to spend money (especially others), are not afraid to hustle for money, not afraid to gamble for money. Most are afraid to manage money. A famous General named Colin Powell was viewed by his men, during the Viet Nam era, as one of the most courageous men they knew. This was because during parachuting from planes he would always jump first. After the instructions were clear and double checking the equipment, without hesitation he would be out of the plane- gone. Unknown to the men that served under him, he never completely got over the fear of jumping. But he knew if the fellow before him failed, the fear could freeze him as well as the others under him. So he got his jump over with as quick as possible. He appeared prepared, fearless, and in command. That's how General Powell faced fear… he faced it while doing what he was trained to do and he did it without hesitation.

False Evidence Appearing Real

Overcoming fear is developed through training, discipline, being prepared to live with the outcome of our actions and being willing
to fail and paying close attention to failure in order to turn the experience into an asset. Yes you heard me right. Are you afraid to fail, afraid to fall, ashamed of looking stupid or inadequate? An acronym for

fear is false evidence appearing real. Appearances can be deceiving. Observation is a good teacher. Study the object of your apprehension; nature is full of creatures of habit. Most occurrences are grounded in the a-b-c's or 1-2-3's. Learn the fundamentals of money like the fundamentals of chess. There is a three-move opening in chess that can win (end) the game if your opponent is ignorant of the strategy. The three fundaments of money (in my opinion) is to earn some, save some and invest some.

Financial fear is rampant in impoverished communities. Hard working people will not contribute to their 401-K incentives. They fail to form the habit of consistently saving. Many will not look for crafts or hobbies that could be turned into extra cash. Most of us will not study finances for ourselves or attempt to master a specific trade. If you can read, nothing can be totally hidden from you. Are you afraid to fail or are you afraid to think? Both can be catastrophic to one's wellbeing. It has been said that, "Most people are one idea away from a million dollars." Know this about money; Money will not manage itself. Use the Colin Powell principle. Carefully go over the instructions, double check the safety precautions…then jump.

Chapter II

IGNORANCE

"The poor you'll have with you always" ~ *Jesus Christ*
"…But it shouldn't be the same poor." ~ *Walter Aikens*

Ignorance is not a very popular word in many circles today. The root of the word is ignore. It does not mean stupid, dumb, or asinine. It means to refuse to take notice of, to reject as ungrounded. The synonym is to reject. In today's challenging economic times, to ignore the qualities that successfully managing financial concerns entail, to some viewers, may very well appear stupid. To reject as ungrounded, the value of money, seems unconscionable.

War on Poverty

"War on Poverty…" Please. To quote Sean Hannity, a popular radio host, "No poor person ever gave me a job." Also, a popular black activist stated in the 2008 presidential campaign that the word "poverty" was not mentioned once by any candidate black, white or Latino. Why would it be? Poverty is depressing and no candidate wants to bore the Jell-O out of people.

A very wise man once stated, "The poor you'll have with you always." Personally, I don't believe it should be the same poor. Someone should be able to better their lot in life. Someone from the ranks of the poor should be able to pull themselves out of poverty.

But to imply that a society can eliminate the status of poverty (in my opinion) is utter lunacy. "Life, liberty and the pursuit of happiness" is a concept not fully understood by the masses. By the way; an added note of the war concept. The war on terrorism, the war on drugs, and the war on poverty... rarely buy into a concept of a war on anything that does not have a face, a place, or an address. It should be an insult to your intelligence.

What a poverty-stricken person needs is an idea, one that helps raise them out of poverty. Do indigent people get ideas? Of course they do, but many ideas of the poor are ignored (the root word of ignorance) or dismissed as fanciful thoughts that are not taken seriously or are sabotaged by a lack of access to viable resources. An example of a fanciful idea was a joke the writer stated while talking to a personal mentor. The mentor said, "That's a million dollar idea." The writer continued to talk as though it was a joke and the mentor had to reiterate his perception of the joke that was stated, "Walter, that's a million dollar idea."

If he or she does not have an idea, then find someone who has an idea, help that person bring his or her idea, their dream, their vision, into fruition. That person will possibly remember you when they come into their kingdom, maybe they won't. During the course of helping build their idea you should pay close attention to how it's done. Perhaps the day will come when you acquire a novel idea. Perchance you can learn to mimic success.

Not to do this is the epitome of ignorance. The word education means to lead or draw out. Everyone has the option to get an education. Where and to what degree one becomes educated is the key question. Even our prisons have become institutions of higher learning. There is potential in everyone but to harvest that potential will take work.

I once wrote a speech titled, "The Value of Education Versus the Cost of Ignorance." Ironically, the person that inspired the dialogue (or provoked it), was the same person that asked the jaw dropping question, "Why Are You Not Rich?" The individual, in the middle of a discourse made a statement that frankly offended me. He stated quite bluntly, *"A man without an education can't tell me anything about the value of an education."* Another jaw dropping moment. I was incensed, and months went by and I could not get the statement out of my head. Typically when I was particularly offended by my mentor I would write him a letter letting him know how I thought he had stepped over the line, but I did not write a letter on this occasion, but I meditated on the incident. I had spoken to my mentor about a dream I had of me on a stage speaking to an auditorium full of youth. I told him that in the dream, I was chewing them out about staying in school and not undermining their future by not taking education seriously, duplicating mistakes I had made. I shared this dream with my mentor and he had stated, "Walt, you never know what God has in store." Now several years later in a sermon he crushes my dream with, *"A man without an education can't tell me anything about the value of an education."* Now, at this time in my life I held a GED and four college credit hours for passing an English class with a C grade when I was 19 years old. That was it; the extent of my formal education. My mentor recognized in me a love for wisdom, a thirst for knowledge and a willingness to share anything I understood that would benefit others. He told me one day, "Walter, I could see you teaching history in the public school system, you need to go back to school." I thought about what he said and took it to heart. I remembered how difficult school had been for me, how ignorant I felt not being able to comprehend math nor retain information for long periods of time and failing grades. The same man that hurt my feelings with the statement, *"A man without an education can't tell me anything about the value of an education,"* is the same man that encouraged me to go back to school. Do not hide when mentors hurt your sensitivities. Reverse the syllables of mentor and you get the word *torment.* Learn to hear with your heart as well as your head. Know who is for your good and do not be ignorant to wise counsel, even if it stings.

The value of education

After developing a character education curriculum using Chess as an intervention for socially challenged youth, I was contracted to teach the course at a community college to students trying to earn a GED.

As a way to prevent teachers from undoing what I was trying to implement, I was also contracted to train the teachers at the community college on two consecutive Saturdays for two hours and paid three hundred dollars per presentation. Bear in mind that I was instructing teachers on character and class room decorum, though I had no BA or BS degree at all. In fact, I was a high school dropout, former drug addict, and ex-convict. So I figured the three hundred dollars ($300.00) per presentation was not bad for a non-degreed man with an unfavorable background armed with an *idea* that might help enhance character, and instill self-respect in a socially challenged population. After the presentation as I was gathering my material, the coordinator approached me and handed over the check for services rendered. With the envelope in hand, she stated, "We paid you three hundred dollars for your presentation. If you had a degree your presentation would have been worth three thousand dollars. You need to go back to school."

Well, it does not get much clearer than that. I was paid $150.00 per hour and felt good about it. Now, I was being informed that I was receiving one tenth of what individuals with undergraduate degrees would receive. Every individual being trained had a degree except me, yet they hung on every word I shared. The cost of ignorance verses the value of education equaled to a 90% reduction in value at that particular place and time.

The manual the community college used in the class was the one I created and I was paid hourly to teach the class for one semester. I sold the school over one thousand dollars' worth of manuals, made six hundred dollars for teacher training and taught the class for one semester at a base rate for new teachers. Being informed that I received 10% of what the presentation was actually worth (because of a lack of formal education) should give us some indication of the *value of an education*. Now let's examine the cost of ignorance.

The cost of ignorance

After teaching the class on character education at the local institution, the media learned about it and a reporter visited the unique class. To my knowledge this was the first Character Education Course taught on a college campus in the state of North Carolina. The reporter observed the class, interviewed the students who were studying for their GED and wrote a very favorable article on the nature and need of a character education course for the socially challenged. The students were impressed, the school administrators were impressed, and most of the fellow teachers were impressed. The following semester, the school wanted to make it mandatory every student preparing for their GED to take the character education class. In order to make the course a required course, the coding of the course had to be changed from a continuing educational course to some other specific.

When the college submitted the necessary forms to the Board of Community Colleges for the change, the board enquired, "Who will be teaching this new required class?" They were informed by the people trying to implement the course; "The gentleman who developed the course and wrote the manual will be facilitating" and they submitted my name. The board of community colleges contacted the school and informed them, "We can't find the gentleman's credentials on record." The school informed the board that I had no degree to put on file. The board snapped back, "You know no one without a four year degree can teach a mandatory course there." PERIOD.

The school administrator Linda Whitlow delivered the news to me. Though we had grown fond of each other, she informed me of the board's decision and asked, "Mr. Aikens, will you come back when you get a degree?" I asked, "A degree in what?" She said, "A degree in **anything**, we'll hire you with a degree in **anything**." There it was, **the cost of ignorance**. I had developed an effective program, valuable to the school, to the students and to me. However, I was ignorant to the mechanisms that a formal education entailed. I lectured and taught on the purpose of knowledge, the value of character and was ignorant to the fundamentals. Remember, the root word of ignorant is **ignore**, not stupid. Ignorant means you **don't know,** Stupid means you **can't know.** I had to dedicate myself to becoming knowledgeable about education, about real success, about real wealth.

No one should tolerate being ignorant to how wealth is acquired. This is what I've learned about the cost of ignorance; *you can't afford it.*

Chapter III

PROCRASTINATION

"Opportunities are never lost; someone will take the ones you let go by."

Anonymous

If there was ever a robber of dreams it has to be procrastination. It siphons off potential and leaves bright men scratching their heads wondering, "Where did the time go?" It's gone nowhere; it's always "right now." Only your youth, your opportunity to develop has escaped. Monday comes around every Monday. But you, like opportunity will not come around as often, because of procrastination.

Procrastinate: *Pro* = to move forward; *Cras* = tomorrow; *Crastinus* = of tomorrow.

Someone said, "It's a shame that youth is wasted on the young." Not managing time is detrimental and virtually fatal to dreams. A person capable of managing time has the potential to manage money. If he can manage time and money he can manage wealth. Remember: money, you can always replace, time - never. So it's important that if one is to truly manage riches one must break the propensity to procrastinate. One must understand that *"Everything is seasonal."* There is a time and place for everything.

The key is not to be caught out of season. Fruit should not be picked early (it will be hard and bitter). It should not hang on the limb too long (it will be subject to rot and parasites). It should be picked in due season and enjoyed, some should be preserved for the lean years that may come, but the procrastinator will come to poverty.

How does one break the propensity to procrastinate? Gathering a true appreciation for time is critical. Most people put off things until they *feel* like doing it. Feelings shift and change like the wind and because of that, are fairly unreliable. In my counseling practice I encourage my clients to address three factors of daily life; *faith, facts and feelings,* which are constantly beckoning us to attend to them. *Feelings* have the loudest voice, and therefore hog our attention. *Facts* can get fairly loud especially when habitually neglected. *Faith* rarely yells. As a matter of *fact*, faith usually whispers. As one matures they usually recognize that youth can be spent like loose pocket change, and when it's time to cash out, we come up short. Many are not willing to accept the blame for our abuse of time. We feel like we were robbed and make a thousand different excuses of why it's not our fault. This day belongs to you, all twenty four hours of it. If you consistently ignore significant parts of your day, an imbalance will occur. Perhaps very subtle and insidious, but most certainly an imbalance will come to be.

We put things off because we don't *feel* like doing it *right now*. Or we don't see the importance of completing what we start in a timely fashion.

Once you get a reputation of not finishing things on time and below a quality standard, you will be called on less and less to participate in meaningful endeavors. Life will proceed past you and you will be rendered insignificant. This will haunt the procrastinator and they will be labeled a great waster of time. "Never put off till tomorrow, what you can do today." Does tomorrow ever come? Or are we constantly fixed in the perpetual present, promised to this "here and now." Remember time is mapped out to benefit man's progression toward maturity. Most people do not prepare to grow old, though it is ingrained in our biological make up. Then when our youth is gone, we find we have not looked ahead and prepared to sustain our old age. Procrastination is the monster you create, and you are Doctor Frankenstein.

Recommended reading; "How to Live on Twenty Four Hours a Day." John Wayne said, "Tomorrow comes to us around midnight. It comes to us pure and clean. And it hopes that we've learned something from yesterday."

Chapter IV

A LACK OF DISCIPLINE

"I love learning, but I don't always like being taught!"
Winston Churchill

How did the word discipline get such a nasty reputation? "Don't dis me, man!" was a popular phrase in the 80's. Right about the time crack cocaine invaded our social consciousness. It meant "don't disrespect." To dismiss someone publicly could bring a firestorm of repercussions. It appears we have become a society that is poised to bring swift retribution for any slight against our perceived self-worth. To function in today's world full of poverty, conflict, chaos and crime, will require that one has the discipline to learn **the art of cultivating a social intelligence.**

The truth of the matter is that discipline belongs in the arena of academia, military, or martial arts more so than the criminal or juvenile justice system. A lack of discipline is responsible for unfinished, incomplete, half done, falling short endeavors that become grotesque monuments of failure. *Finish what you start,* is one of the tenets of Tae Kwon Do. That's why it is considered a discipline, followers of Christ were called disciples.

The unenlightened that feel they are qualified to discipline others are less familiar with the true meaning of the word. Discipline: *disciplina* = teaching, learning, instruction. If these three aspects of discipline are summed up into a single concept it may encompass (in a word) *educate*. Teaching, learning, instruction, is designed to bring out the best in you. There are hidden talents in all of us, but to discover (to reveal) the true value of a thing is rarely easy. What surfaces easily is not well hidden.

Being teachable has never been a given by the masses. Our educational system is ill equipped to effectively cultivate the talent latent in the minds of the youth today. There are different learning styles and genius untapped right in our midst. Without the discipline to mine the precious elements deep within the human phenomena and the patience to recognize value tangled within the human condition, unfulfilled dreams will haunt the graveyards of the world like shadowy ghosts.

To become disciplined, one has to address the question; are you teachable? If one is not teachable, then what *should* be discipline, becomes punishment. What *should* be teaching now becomes correction. Men are notorious for trying to assemble things without reading the instructions. I was raised by a man that was removed from school in the second grade around 1935. During the sixties I would observe him attempting to assemble toys at Christmas. He was quite brilliant (though I did not recognize it at the time).

I must have been about 11 when watching him struggle, I started to pick up the instructions that came in the box and started to make suggestions; "this may go here, and that may go like this." I became an asset to him. If you can read the instructions, you can put almost anything together. Nothing can be hidden from the man who can read the map. Learning to read (and with comprehension) will require *discipline*. Procrastination is a clear obstacle to developing discipline. Discipline will require commitment, dedication and perseverance.

School was rarely easy for me. In college, I developed a formula that made getting through a semester more agreeable. Dealing with adult Attention Deficit Hyperactivity Disorder (ADHD), I was easily distracted. Every sound grabbed my ear, the slightest movement caught my eye, every thought that ran through my mind wanted to rush out of my mouth. To avoid falling victim to my distractions, I knew I needed to be at the front of the classroom. In large classes in order to guarantee my seat, I developed the discipline of coming to class early. Positioning myself in the optimum vantage point required for me to succeed was important. Once, I was running late and a female student was in my usual seat. I was so thrown off my pattern, I made an open joke to the class that, that particular seat was reserved. I determined in school never to miss a class, school was too important.

There was a time right after spring break, the weather was beautiful, and I was riding around just enjoying life when it dawned on me… "What do I usually do at this time on this particular day?" Oh My!!! I'm supposed to be in class. One and a half hours late, mentally I was out to lunch. I rushed over to the school to find class had just ended. A few of the students were still there and I apologized to the instructor. The remaining students informed me that my seat remained empty the entire class because they never knew me to miss a day and knew I always sat in the same seat. Discipline creates habit. Discipline feeds habit. One must carefully choose the habit one desires. Consistency paves the road to becoming disciplined. Discipline first requires one to start with the end in mind. Set a goal, see it in your mind and draw it out on paper if you must. Discipline secondly requires one to count up the cost. Are you willing to make the sacrifice? Discipline thirdly will require you to attempt to maintain a consistent pace towards *finishing what you start*. This is what brings discipline to be viewed as an art form. Find a successful mentor and consistently follow their example. You may not agree with everything they say but observe their propensities, their habits. Ask questions and listen to their answers. If you don't take the bulk of their advice, study their lifestyle, follow them.

There are mentors on the bookshelves of the public library. Great thinkers, men/women of renown and accomplishment. Their minds are now on paper and audio and can be your constant companions.

If we are not disciplined enough to read, study, investigate how money is earned or how wealth is acquired, poverty will be your personal companion, debt your down fall and financial failure your own fault.

Chapter V

THE LANGUAGE OF WEALTH

"Learning has loops and every loop has a language."
Walter Aikens

There is a language to the culture of becoming financially independent. Remember my maxim; Learning has loops and every loop has a language. There are fourteen words that many neglect to clearly define and when riches present their access, we are unable to exploit the sustenance. Ignorance of these factors strip many of their ability to manage riches. They are as follows; **Capital, Collateral, Currency, Debt, Estate, Mint, Money, Profit, Rich, Talent, Tariff, Tax, Value, and Wealth.**

Talent [talente] was originally *a unit of money*. Now it is considered a mental or physical aptitude, natural or acquired ability. Some dictionaries say a superior natural endowment or ability before they define it as a variable unit of weight and money used in ancient Greece. The Greek word: **TALANTON** referred to *an amount of money*. An ingot of gold weighing 57 pounds was a *talanton* during the commerce of the Greeks during the time of Homer.

Because you have talent (money) does not mean you have a gift (exceptional aptitude or ability) and because you are gifted (exceptional aptitude or ability) does not mean you can automatically turn it into talent (money).

Wealth [weal]; is the abundance of valuable resources or valuable material possessions. Wealth: from weal (Old English) / Money; epithet; from Moneta (Lat.) Juno. Moneta was one of the titles of the Roman goddess Juno. In the temple dedicated to her the Romans minted their money

Capital is a type of good that can be consumed now, but if consumption is deferred, an increased supply of consumable goods is likely to be available later. In *financial economics*, capital refers to any assets used to make money, as opposed to assets used for personal enjoyment or consumption. This is an important distinction because two people can disagree sharply about the value of personal assets.

Collateral is a borrower's pledge of specific property to a lender, to secure repayment of a loan.

Currency in the most specific use of the word refers to money in any form when in actual use or circulation as a medium of exchange, particularly circulating banknotes (cash) and coins.

Estate - *to stand*, a term in common law for a person's property, entitlements and obligations.

Mint - a facility for manufacturing coins.

Money - Money is a tool that is used to barter life's comforts. According to Webster's New Collegiate Dictionary money is: *something generally accepted as a medium of exchange, a measure of value, or a means of payment.*

Profit is the return to an owner of capital goods or natural resources in any productive pursuit involving labor, or a return on bonds and money invested in capital markets. Also, bonds and money invested in capital markets

Rich is a prehistoric German word borrowed from the Celtics. Rich, Reich, and Royal are all related to the word kingdom, royal, (possessing or controlling great wealth). Related words are wealthy which stresses the possession of property and intrinsically valuable things. It suggests affluence; suggests prosperity and an increasing wealth. Opulent suggests lavish expenditure and a display of great wealth.

Value - to be of worth, be strong. From the same root as valor/ strong, brave. *It takes courage to protect valuables/manage riches.*

Tax - charge, onerous, to feel, censure, touch.

Tariff - A schedule of duties (price/charge) imposed by a government on imported or in some countries exported goods.

Chapter VI

MINT CONDITION

"The mint makes it first, it is up to you to make it last."
Evan Esar

Here I will share a presentation from a commencement speech for a graduating class. "In MINT Condition" was the title of my discourse. At the end of my speech, a very attractive Caucasian female dressed in business black approached me before I left the stage and said, "That (speech) could be a chapter in a book." Then she asked me something that really drove home the power of the spoken word. She asked, "Can I have your notes?" I looked at the three sheets of paper in my hand and hesitated. There were last minute notes I had written around the margin. By giving her the speech, I would not have access to the last minute addendum. I told her that if she left me her contact information I would try to get a cleaned up copy of the lecture to her. Here we are years later and her words appeared to have rung true. That was in 2009 and I think it fitting to insert it here in Why Are You Not Rich?

I opened the speech with a question. I asked the group, "If I had to send someone from this group, this room, this body of people out there into the world to represent the whole of us;

could I send you? PAUSE. If the answer to the question is no: then why not? PAUSE. If not you, then who? Take a good look around you. Look at your friends, your associates, your competitors, your adversaries. *Look*... Who could you send, who would you send, who could you trust to represent your good name, your perspective, your point of view in your absence? *Be careful...,* you are about to recommend them. You are about to link your name with their name. In the grand scheme of things your name is all that you have.

Mint is a plant. Its oil is used in medicine, (physical healing). It is used as a food, in teas, and candies, (nourishment). It is used for its aromatic fragrance in Aroma therapy, (mental and emotional healing). Many of you will be like sweet mint in the areas you travel to, in the positions you hold in life. You will be medicinal to many you come in contact with like a precious ointment prepared by the hand of the universal good to enhance health and longevity. You will bring freshness to the endeavors you touch.

Others of you will bring nourishment to situations that are starving for change, for leadership, for vitality, for vigor, for vision. Many of you will feed thousands that thirst and hunger for a destiny because they are lost without a true sense of purpose.

Then there are those of you who will come as a sweet fragrance bringing healing to feeble hearts and troubled minds that need to know that there is hope for an ailing society.

You are that fragrance refreshing life and lives that are stiff with yesteryears exploits, you are the future's voice and I hear the song of your choir. It is the song of destiny, it is the song of determination powered by your thrust, it is your world and you are more than capable of conquering whatever challenge presents itself before you. Will life be fair? (Don't be silly) NO, life will not be fair. Will there be pain? Ahh!!! Yes. Are you up for the challenge? Oh yes. ***Developing character always leaves a scar... always.*** By the very definition of the word; character/ carve / cutting/ impression. **If you find a man that has no battle scars, you have found a man with no character.** But there is another meaning to the word mint. A mint also refers to a place where money is made or minted, particularly coins. There they are stamped with an image and information. They are put under tremendous pressure because they are of such hard material, that it requires great pressure to leave the desired impression. The precious metal (you) has been tempered, hardened, heated and treated because it (you) has been built to last.

At this point in your life, you have been put under a lot of pressure. Some of you have been very hard to work with because that is your nature. *Some of you have been almost impossible to work with simply because you were hard headed.* But now you are here in mint condition. But in order to fulfill its destiny, in order to achieve its design *you* must be put into circulation before you are truly considered currency.

The word currency and curriculum are derived from the same Latin root; to run, to race. Currency; is a flowing/medium of exchange. Curriculum; is a course of study. ***Knowledge and money are that closely related.*** You are the currency of this nation's future. But to be put in circulation means money (you) will be handled, passed around, spent, you will be saved, lost, found, forgotten, lent, set aside for special occasions, and discovered in some of the darnest places. **THAT'S WHAT HAPPENS TO CURRENCY.** But it's not personal. That's what you are here for. That is why you are here. **This is not personal, this is business. We are not investing** *in you* **we are** *investing you.* You are our hope, you are our savings, and you are our medium of exchange for goods.

Newly minted money has several things (characteristics) that are interestingly very similar to you. Four things currency has that you share are 1.) Money has a history; there is a date stamped on it. 2.) Money has an image stamped on it, typically of someone or something held in high esteem or someone highly honored. 3.) Money (U.S. minted) has a motto/creed on it. Something that keeps us   focused on our principles, our purpose. 4.) Money (U.S. minted) has a statement of faith. It tells the world where the trust of this great nation lies (IN GOD WE TRUST).

You like currency have a history, a very valuable history. You have a date of birth. If you have a birth certificate, you have already made history.

Note this; everyone is going to make history, but some of us are going to shape history. Your birth certificate certifies that you have made history, but are you going to shape history. Everyone will have an opportunity to shape, fashion, or form something of historic value. Remember "opportunities are never lost; someone will take the ones you let go by."

You, also, like currency, have an image; an image that you should protect, that you should honor. Les Brown stated, "When you walk into a room you should fill it with your presence. But when you open your mouth you tell the world who you are."

You, also, like currency, should have a motto/creed; "E Pluribus Unum" Out of many-one. You should have a motto that helps to keep you in line with your mission statement. Please tell me you have a mission statement. My personal motto is a bit wild, selfish, and maybe a little arrogant, but I like it. *"This day belongs to me. It is the greatest day of my life- because it is the only day that I have. If you are kind I will loan you a moment. If you are unkind you are the wrong kind and you have no right to waste my time."* The fourth and last thing that currency has that you should have is a statement of faith. U.S. minted currency states, "In God We Trust." My statement of faith is, "All others pay cash." No, that is just a joke. My personal statement of faith is,

"For with God, nothing shall be impossible" Luke 1:37 KJV

But I must voice my concerns towards some of our newly minted currency (you, my younger readers). I am concerned when you are more concerned about showing me your underwear, than your understanding of your potential. I am concerned when you are more concerned about showing me your attitude than your aptitude for success. I am concerned when you are more concerned with showing the world your disrespect more than your self-respect... I'm just a little concerned. I encourage you to be mindful.

In closing, I am going to share with you four things one would do well to be mindful of. If you intend to control real wealth in your life time or desire to live a life that will not cause you or your loved ones great financial hardship, one should mind the following four things;

MIND: *Mind your mind.* Your mind is reality's link to heaven and earth. Do not cause it any unnecessary harm. No self-inflicted wounds, please. Your imagination will shape worlds beyond my wildest stretch because you are the future's voice; please, *please* have something to say. **Don't** do the wild things to enhance your perception of life, just live and life will enhance itself, trust me. Life takes no prisoners and you may want to be sober when life takes a mad dash across your lane. Mind your mind, your intellect, your reasoning, your discretion, and your rationale. If you mind your mind, you should one day mind your own business (be self-employed). **Avoid recreational drug use or being under the influence**.

Speaking of influence, this is a perfect segue to the second thing one should mind on the journey to success.

INFLUENCE: *Mind your influence.* Influence is a neglected treasure. Many today do not know how to cultivate it or who to cultivate it with. Observe the way students talk to teachers today. Do you hear "yes sir or no madam?" Most do not know how to offer a legitimate apology (because few feel the need to). I am convinced influence is worth more than money. You cultivate influence by cultivating character. Gentlemen are rarely found today; someone that says "excuse me" even when you bumped into them, one that will get the door for a man or woman that appears to need help with packages (and offers to carry the packages for the lady). Sharpen your power of persuasion and maintain your good name by committing random acts of kindness on purpose. Influence should be fluid. It should flow from you and nourish/nurture those in your immediate environment. When people respect you, they are glad to see you coming. When they fear you, they are glad to see you leaving. Cultivate influence at all cost. Talent may get you in the door, character will keep you in the door, but influence will take you to the top floor. Constant self-cultivation is a personal daily goal. **Mind your influence.**

In a certain culture, money was referred to as *dead presidents.* You have heard phrases like, *"It's all about the Benjamin's."* Benjamin Franklin was never president but he *influenced* presidents. Alexander Hamilton was never president he was secretary of the *treasury.*

I challenged a group of high school seniors that I could tell if they had started to cultivate influence. "If you cannot name three individuals (outside of your family members) that could or would give you a letter of recommendation after four years of high school, you have not cultivated influence." What you know may get you in the door, but who you know will get you up the stairs. Talent (as we know it) is not enough. To be in mint condition without character means you will not be in circulation long. Remember; currency flows in a current.

NAME: *Mind your name.* Your name is the greatest capital you will ever possess; protect it at all cost. Try not to bring unwarranted shame upon it, it affects more than just you.

Be mindful of your presentation, your choice of words in public, your associations, and your temperament. All should be guarded and watched over diligently for they will add a stench or a fragrance to your name. When you are dead, buried and gone your name will still be above ground. A name has the capacity to live on. Your name is not an accident. Part of your name is a gift (first name) and part is on loan (last name). The word *name* means *authority.* When someone is introduced to you and they have to ask you to repeat your name more than twice, one of two things has happened. Either you are not sure of who you are, or you don't speak effective English. My name (authority) is ***Walter Anthony Aikens.*** I slow down when saying my name upon being introduced. I don't rush past my name during an introduction.

You never know who is present, who is watching, or who is listening. Your name should make a statement. It is designed to show or state your authority in the earth. Your profession, your calling, your purpose for being, why you are here, are all wrapped in your name. Walter is of German Origin, meaning the *Conquering Warrior* or *Ruler of People*. Anthony is of Latin origin, meaning *Priceless/ Incapable of being estimated/ Wise Counselor*. *Aiken* (from the word acorn) is English meaning *made of oak*. In the Yoruba language *Akins* means *brave*.

So the statement of my name is *The Conquering Warrior Is Priceless and Possesses the Seed of Great Strength*. Protect your authority, guard your good name. Your name should distinguish you from those who do not know their destiny. Make a statement heard through your deeds to mankind. Make your name count. Study Alfred Nobel if you want to know how to redeem your name…Hint: *Nobel Peace Prize*.

TIME: *Mind your time*. Your time is priceless. You can invest it, or you can waste it, but you cannot keep it. Time has no reverse gear. Youth may be on your side but time is not your friend. There are seven teenage years (thirteen through nineteen). Seven is the number of completion, maturity, perfection, and wholeness. When the window closes, one can never go back to being a teenager again. You may act like a fourteen year old but the world has certain expectations of every adult. Failure to live up to certain social criteria can be embarrassing and very painful for you and others who may depend on your maturity. Time is not a game.

Games are played in the confines of time but time is never played in the confines of games. In other words; there is no "time out." During the teen-age years it would be an excellent time to teach a young person about the principles of finance. *Personal story~* as of this writing I am raising a 17-year-old daughter who has just landed her first job at a restaurant. She is also interested in culinary arts. She agreed to tithe (that is her option) and agreed to save ten percent of her check (pay yourself first or second in her case) and put aside five percent for miscellaneous concerns; offering, to cover a friend who may come up short for a movie etc. etc. Well, she and her mother have a direct deposit account the two of them have access to. It appears very difficult for my daughter (with the help of her mother) to bring me the 25% of her take home pay.

I believe that one should separate what is to be saved and especially what is to be presented before God (do not put all your eggs in one basket). I have had to become adamant in expressing the importance of honoring her agreement. She does not see the importance now of monitoring this simple budget, but if it is done consistently the awareness (opposite of ignorance) will sink in. Remember; **Youth may be on your side, but time is not your friend.** I love the way John Wayne put it. *"Tomorrow comes to us around midnight. It comes to us pure and clean. And it hopes that we've learned something, from yesterday."*

Mix the study of history and money as a hobby. Study everyone that is on a dollar bill; From George Washington to Salmon P. Chase. Well that might be a little much, but everyone should study from George Washington to Benjamin Franklin. You must cultivate your mind, cultivate your influence, guard and protect your name as rare treasure and invest your time in worthy endeavors that will reap an enormous harvest to be added to your legacy. You are in mint condition. But without character you will not be in circulation long. Remember currency flows in a current. Why would one desire to control wealth (become rich)? Good Question. There is a parable of a city that was in trouble and a poor man offered a suggestion that preserved the city. Yet after the catastrophe had passed, the city ceased honoring the indigent man because he was still poor. He helped save the city but choose not to alleviate his own plight. Poor Richard said, "Three friends are sure. An old wife, an old dog, and ready money."

You are in mint condition, you are the currency of this nation's future, we are no longer investing in you; *we are investing you.* So you mind your MIND, mind your INFLUENCE, mind your NAME, and mind your TIME.

Remember the lifespan of a moment is incalculable. Once it has passed, it cannot return.

Now… it's your move.

EPILOGUE

"Reading has brought wealth. Writing has brought riches."
Walter Aikens

Wealth and riches are close cousins, not twins. The first wealth is health. A sound mind and fit body are key components to acquiring riches. The word *key* is derived from an ancient concept meaning *solution*. My library shelves have a wealth of knowledge that I am at liberty to access at will and others may access after I am no longer able to (or have a need to) access the information myself *(Wealth)*. The sales of my book, *The Purpose of Knowledge: What Every Human Should Know*, supplied the *capital* that helped qualify me and my wife to buy a home *(Riches)*. Wealth rhymes with health. Health is considered the first wealth. Soundness of mind, body and emotions are assets. If a person has good health and a sound mind, there really should be no excuse for habitual failure. The only other ingredients needed (at that point) are motivation and focus.

So here we are. At the end but still addressing the original question encountered at the beginning. Why are you not rich? You have no idea? Well, therein may lie the problem. YOU HAVE NO *IDEA*. If the statement is true; "Most people are *one* idea away from being a millionaire…" then it would behoove you to think. Find an idea, borrow one, or improve something already in existence. If you do not know what to think on, try this; stop - look - and listen. If you find a need and fill it, you have the potential to become indispensable. Benjamin Franklin saw dirt being tracked into his place of business. He asked a local handy man if he would keep the area swept in front of his business.

Well, the dirt ended up at the edge of the two businesses on either side of Franklin's property. Those business owners eventually employed the same man to keep their area clean. The profession of street sweeper was invented. STOP, LOOK, LISTEN. I know self-employed window washers driving Cadillacs.

Why Are You Not Rich? By the time a man turns forty, this may be a legitimate question that he should be prepared to answer one way or the other, particularly in a capitalist society. This work addresses four barriers the writer has acknowledged were personal limitations. So, you now know the specters of the writer's want/lack: ***Fear, Ignorance, Procrastination and a Lack of Discipline.*** What are your restrictions, your challenges, your excuses? Some of you have an idea that you are not sure of, not certain if it's viable, an idea that you have allowed to linger in its infancy. The lifespan of a moment is incalculable, slips by subtlety. But over time, moments become seconds that turn into minutes, then hours, days, months, years, and eventually a lifetime. ***Your*** lifetime. If you are reading this message, the only certainty you possess is that, *you are literally here for the moment.* Now, it's your move.

BONUS ADDENDUM: Benjamin Franklin's autobiography is considered to be possibly the nation's first self-help book. Its rumored he may have been the nation's first (self-made) millionaire. If that's true he appears to have earned the right to be on the 100 dollar bill. The name Franklin is connected with land ownership and money (francs/money- lin/land). A bonus feature of his thoughts on riches are at the end of this book.

Benjamin Franklin, *The Way to Wealth* (1758). [*The classic Franklin summary of his advice from Poor Richard's Almanac.*]

"In 1732 I first published my Almanac under the name of *Richard Saunders*; it was continued by me about twenty-five years, and commonly called *Poor Richard's Almanac*. I endeavored to make it both entertaining and useful, and it accordingly came to be in such demand, that I reaped considerable profit from it, vending annually near ten thousand. And observing that it was generally read, (scarce any neighborhood in the province being without it,) I considered it as a proper vehicle for conveying instruction among the common people, who bought scarcely any other books. I therefore filled all the little spaces, that occurred between the remarkable days in the Calendar, with proverbial sentences, chiefly such as inculcated industry and frugality, as the means of procuring wealth, and thereby securing virtue; it being more difficult for a man in want to act always honestly, as (to use here one of those proverbs) *It is hard for an empty sack to stand upright.*"

***

Courteous Reader,

I have heard, that nothing gives an author so great pleasure as to find his works respectfully quoted by others. Judge, then, how much I must have been gratified by an incident I am going to relate, to you. I stopped my horse lately, where a great number of people were collected at an auction of merchants' goods. The hour of the sale not being come, they were conversing on the badness of the times; and one of the company called to a plain, clean, old man, with white locks, "Pray, Father Abraham, what think you of the times? Will not these heavy taxes quite ruin the country? How shall we ever be able to pay them? What would you advise us to?" Father Abraham stood up, and replied, "If you would have my Advice, I will give it you in short; for *a word to the wise is enough,* as Poor Richard says." They joined in desiring him to speak his mind, and gathering round him, he proceeded as follows.

"Friends," said he, "the taxes are indeed very heavy, and, if those laid on by the government were the only ones we had to pay, we might more easily discharge them; but we have many others, and much more grievous to some of us. We are taxed twice as much by our idleness, three times as much by our pride, and four times as much by our folly; and from these taxes the commissioners cannot ease or deliver us, by allowing an abatement. However, let us hearken to good advice, and something may be done for us; *God helps them that help themselves,* as Poor Richard says...

"I. It would be thought a hard government, that should tax its people one-tenth part of their time, to be employed in its service; but idleness taxes many of us much more; sloth, by bringing on diseases, absolutely shortens life. *Sloth, like rust, consumes faster than labor wears; while the used key is always bright,* as Poor Richard says. *But dost thou love life, then do not squander time, for that is the stuff life is made of,* as Poor Richard says. How much more than is necessary do we spend in sleep, forgetting, that *The sleeping fox catches no poultry,* and that *There will be sleeping enough in the grave,* as Poor Richard says.

"*If time be of all things the most precious, wasting time must be,* as Poor Richard says, the greatest prodigality; since, as he elsewhere tells us, *Lost time is never found again; and what we call time enough, always proves little enough.* Let us then up and be doing, and doing to the purpose; so by diligence shall we do more with less perplexity. *Sloth makes all things difficult, but industry all easy;* and *He that riseth late must trot all day, and shall scarce overtake his business at night;* while *Laziness travels so slowly, that Poverty soon overtakes him. Drive thy business, let not that drive thee; and early to bed, and early to rise, makes a man healthy, wealthy, and wise,* as Poor Richard says.

"So what signifies wishing and hoping for better times? We may make these times better, if we bestir ourselves. *Industry need not wish, and he that lives upon hopes will die fasting. There are no gains without pains; then help, hands, for I have no lands;* or, if I have, they are smartly taxed.

He that hath a trade hath an estate; and he that hath a calling, hath an office of profit and honor, as Poor Richard says; but then the trade must be worked at, and the calling followed, or neither the estate nor the office will enable us to pay our taxes. If we are industrious, we shall never starve; for, *At the working man's house hunger looks in, but dares not enter.* Nor will the bailiff or the constable enter, for *Industry pays debts, while despair increaseth them.* What though you have found no treasure, nor has any rich relation left you a legacy, *Diligence is the mother of good luck, and God gives all things to industry. Then plough deep while sluggards sleep, and you shall have corn to sell and to keep.* Work while it is called to-day, for you know not how much you may be hindered to-morrow. *One, to-day is worth two to-morrows,* as Poor Richard says; and further, *Never leave that till to-morrow, which you can do to-day.* If you were a servant, would you not be, ashamed that a good master should catch you idle? Are you then your own master? Be ashamed to catch yourself idle, when there is so much to be done for yourself, your family, your country, and your king. Handle your tools without mittens; remember, that *The cat in gloves catches no mice*, as Poor Richard says.

It is true there is much to be done, and perhaps you are weak-handed; but stick to it steadily, and you will see great effects; for *Constant dropping wears away stones;* and *By diligence and patience the mouse ate in two the cable; and Little strokes fell great oaks.*

"Methinks I hear some of you say, 'Must a man afford himself no leisure?'

I will tell thee, my friend, what Poor Richard says, *Employ thy time well, if thou meanest to gain leisure; and, since thou art not sure of a minute, throw not away an hour.* Leisure is time for doing something useful; this leisure the diligent man will obtain, but the lazy man never; *for A life of leisure and a life of laziness are two things. Many, without labor, would live by their wits only, but they break for want of stock*; whereas industry gives comfort, and plenty, and respect. *Fly pleasures, and they will follow you. The diligent spinner has a large shift; and now I have a sheep and a cow, everybody bids me good morrow.*

"II. But with our industry we must likewise be steady, settled, and careful, and oversee our own affairs with our own eyes, and not trust too much to others; . . . Trusting too much to others' care is the ruin of many; for *In the affairs of this world men are saved, not by faith, but by the want of it*, . . .

"III. So much for industry, my friends, and attention to one's own business; but to these we must add frugality if we would make our industry more certainly successful. A man may, if he knows not bow to save as be gets, keep his nose all his life to the grindstone, and die not worth a groat at last.", *A fat kitchen makes a lean will*; and

Many estates are spent in the getting, since women for tea forsook spinning and knitting, and men for punch forsook hewing and splitting.

If you would be wealthy, think of saving as well as of getting. The Indies have not made Spain rich, because her outgoes are greater than her incomes.

"Away then with your expensive follies, and you will not then have so much cause to complain of bard times, heavy taxes, and chargeable families; for *Women and wine, game and deceit, Make the wealth small and the want great.*

And further, *What maintains one vice would bring up two children.* You may think, perhaps, that a little tea, or a little punch now and then, -diet a little more costly, clothes a little finer, and a little' entertainment now and then, can be no great matter; but remember, *Many a little makes a mickle.* Beware of little expenses; *A small leak will sink a great ship*, as Poor Richard says and again, . . .

Here you are all got together at this sale of fineries and knick-knacks.

You call them *goods*; but, if you do not take care, they will prove *evils* to some of you. You expect they will be sold cheap, and perhaps they may for less than they cost; but, if you have no occasion for them, they must be dear to you. Remember what Poor Richard says; *Buy what thou. hast no need of, and ere long thou shalt sell thy necessaries.* . . . Many a one, for the sake of finery on the back, have gone with a hungry belly and half-starved their families. *Silks and satins, scarlet and velvets, put out the kitchen fire*, as Poor Richard says.

"These are not the necessaries of life; they can scarcely be called the conveniences; and yet, only because they look pretty, how many want to have them!"

By these, and other extravagances, the genteel are reduced to poverty, and forced to borrow of those whom they formerly despised, but who, through industry and frugality, have maintained their standing; in which case it appears plainly, that *A ploughman on his legs is higher than a gentleman on his knees*, as Poor Richard says. . . . But this they might have known before, if they had taken his advice. *If you would know the value of money, go and try to borrow some; for, he that goes a borrowing goes a sorrowing*, as Poor Richard says; . . . .

"But what madness must it be to *run in debt* for these superfluities? We are offered by the terms of this sale, six months' credit; and that, perhaps, has induced some of us to attend it, because we cannot spare the ready money, and hope now to be fine without it.

But, ah! think what you do when, you run in debt you give to another power over your liberty. If you cannot pay at the time, you will be ashamed to see your creditor; you will be in fear when you speak to him; you will make poor, pitiful, sneaking excuses, and, by degrees, come to lose your veracity, and sink into base, downright lying; for *The second vice is lying, the first is running in debt*, as Poor Richard says; . . .

"What would you think of that prince, or of that government, who should issue an edict forbidding you to dress like a gentleman or gentlewoman, on pain of imprisonment or servitude?

Would you not say that you were free, have a right to dress as you please, and that such an edict would be a breach of your privileges, and such a government tyrannical? And yet you are about to put yourself under such tyranny, when you run in debt for such dress! Your creditor has authority, at his pleasure, to deprive you of your liberty, by confining you in jail till you shall be able to pay him. When you have got your bargain, you may, perhaps, think little of payment; but, as Poor Richard says, *Creditors have better memories than debtors; creditors are a superstitious sect, great observers of set days and time*s. . . .

"IV. This doctrine, my friends, is reason and wisdom; but, after all, do not depend too much upon your own industry, and frugality, and prudence, though excellent things; for they may all be blasted, without the blessing of Heaven; and, therefore, ask that blessing humbly, and be not uncharitable to those that at present seem to want it, but comfort and help them Remember, Job suffered, and was afterwards prosperous."

Source: *The Works of Benjamin Franklin*. Edited by Jared Sparks. Vol. 2. (Boston, 1836), 2:92-103.

About the Author

Walter A. Aikens was born and lives in Greensboro, North Carolina. He is married and has three children. After rising above hardship and challenges early in life, Walter found the strength to rise above his circumstances. In addition to having an Associate Degree in Biblical Studies from Evangel Bible College, Walter has an entrepreneurial spirit and holds a First Degree Black Belt in Tae Kwon Do from Greensboro Black Belt Academy. He holds a Bachelor of Arts Degree in Sociology with a concentration in Criminal Justice from Shaw University. He earned a Master's Degree in Clinical Mental Health Counseling with a concentration in Addictions from North Carolina Agricultural and Technical State University. Walter founded a nonprofit mentoring program called the *Hero Factor Inc.* that targeted at risk youth from single parent homes with a focus on character development and school dropout prevention. You will often find his heart in causes that assist troubled youth and individuals in advancing above their current circumstances. Other books by Walter include Scattered Pieces of a Broken Dream, The Purpose of Knowledge: What Every Human Should Know, The Lifespan of a Moment, and The Art of Cultivating Social Intelligence: A Course in Character Development.

~ NOTES ~

Why Are You Not Rich?

Why Are You Not Rich?

Why Are You Not Rich?

Why Are You Not Rich?

Why Are You Not Rich?

Why Are You Not Rich?

~ NOTES ~

Why Are You Not Rich?

Why Are You Not Rich?

~ NOTES ~

Why Are You Not Rich?

Why Are You Not Rich?

Why Are You Not Rich?

Why Are You Not Rich?

www.ingramcontent.com/pod-product-compliance
Lightning Source LLC
LaVergne TN
LVHW041206080426
835508LV00008B/816